This book belongs to

_____

If you could have any fictional character start at your school on Monday, who would it be? What would you do together?

If you could go back to being 2 years old, with the same brain you have now, would you do it?
Why, or why not?

_____

_____

_____

_____

_____

_____

_____

_____

_____

_____

_____

_____

_____

_____

_____

_____

What would you do if you found out your next-door neighbor was an alien? Report them to the authorities? Befriend them?

What would you do if your best friend asked you to help cover up a crime they committed?

_____

_____

_____

_____

_____

_____

_____

_____

_____

_____

_____

_____

_____

_____

_____

_____

_____

_____

Do you think kids should be made to go to school? What could the alternative be?

If you could have $10k right now, or $1,000,000
when you're 40, which would you choose? Why?

Describe the house you'd build if you had an unlimited budget and could go anywhere in the world.

_____

_____

_____

_____

_____

_____

_____

_____

_____

_____

_____

_____

_____

_____

_____

_____

_____

_____

_____

You wake up and you're in charge of the country.
What's the first law you change, and why?

You have $10k to spend on improving your school. How do you spend it?

If you had to lose one of your senses, which would you choose? Why?

You're able to read people's minds for the day. Do you do it, or would you rather not know? Whose mind would you read?

_____

_____

_____

_____

_____

_____

_____

_____

_____

_____

_____

_____

_____

Would you rather spend a week alone in an expensive hotel, or a week with all your friends in a cheap hotel?

If you could live inside one song, which would it be? Why?

You can give one item in your bedroom a magical property. Which item do you choose, and what can it do?

_____

_____

_____

_____

_____

_____

_____

_____

_____

_____

_____

_____

_____

_____

_____

A time traveler comes to tell you that there'll be an earthquake in 10 minutes' time. How do you persuade the people around you to take cover?

Would you rather live in the hottest place on Earth, or the coldest? Why?

If you could go back in time two years and tell yourself one thing, what would it be?

Would you rather learn to speak to animals, or learn every language spoken by humans?

You can only eat one food for the rest of your life: pizza. Which toppings do you choose?

_____

_____

_____

_____

_____

_____

_____

_____

_____

_____

_____

_____

_____

_____

_____

_____

What would you do if you opened your front door and found a newborn baby on the doorstep?

If someone made a movie of your life so far, what would happen? Who would play you?

If you could go back and change one event from history, what would it be? How would the world be different as a result?

Would you rather go back in time to see dinosaurs, or to space to meet aliens? Why?

_____

_____

_____

_____

_____

_____

_____

_____

_____

_____

_____

_____

_____

_____

_____

If you could find the cure to one disease, what would it be? Why?

What would you wear if you were invited to walk the catwalk at a fashion show?

Imagine you wake up, and you're the only person on earth. What do you do?

If you could be famous for anything, what would it be? Sports? Art? Music? A scientific discovery?

Imagine you're running your own restaurant. What's the decor like, what do you serve, and what kind of events do you run?

Would you want to be friends with yourself if you were someone else? Why, or why not?

If you could be any fictional character, who would you be, and why?

_____

_____

_____

_____

_____

_____

_____

_____

_____

_____

_____

_____

_____

_____

_____

_____

_____

If you could move into a house of your own right now, would you want to do it? Why?

If you could be the best in the world at any sport, which sport would you choose? Why?

If you could be any animal, which animal would you want to be?

Would you transform your pet (or another animal) into a human if you could? What would they be like? What would you do together?

_____

_____

_____

_____

_____

_____

_____

_____

_____

_____

_____

_____

_____

_____

_____

_____

_____

_____

If you had the ability to see how and when you die, would you want to do it? Why?

_____

_____

_____

_____

_____

_____

_____

_____

_____

_____

_____

_____

_____

_____

_____

_____

Imagine you're designing your own museum.
What's the theme, and what are your exhibits?

Would you rather live in a small apartment in the city, or a mansion in the countryside? Why?

_____

_____

_____

_____

_____

_____

_____

_____

_____

_____

_____

_____

_____

_____

_____

_____

What if you could have a million dollars, but in exchange you could never use the internet again? Would you take it?

Would you rather be banned from going out during the day, or during the night? Why?

_____

_____

_____

_____

_____

_____

_____

_____

_____

_____

_____

_____

_____

_____

_____

_____

If you could have either a personal chef or a personal driver, which would you choose?

If you could get any tattoo or piercing you like with no pain, what would you get?

Would you rather keep your best friend and lose your other friends, or lose your best friend and keep your other friends? Why?

Which 'bad guy' from a film isn't actually that bad, in your opinion? Why?

What's the best thing that could possibly happen to you this week?

_____

_____

_____

_____

_____

_____

_____

_____

_____

_____

_____

_____

_____

_____

_____

_____

Would you rather have a high-paying job, or run a successful business?

What would you do if you woke up in a country where you don't speak the language, with none of your possessions and no idea how you got there?

If you could have one superpower (flying, invisibility, telekinesis, etc), what would it be? Why?

What if you could save the life of someone you know, but in return you'd lose all your memories of them? Would you do it?

If you could open a hotel anywhere in the world, where would it be and what would it be like?

If you could erase all religion from the world, would you do it? Why, or why not?

What's the biggest risk you've ever taken? Did it pay off?

What's the earliest memory you have from childhood?

What's been the best day of your life so far, and why?

What's been the hardest day of your life so far, and why?

Who inspires you the most in life? Why? How can you be more like them?

If you had to celebrate one holiday every single day of the year, which holiday would you choose? Christmas? Halloween? Easter? Why?

What's your favorite thing about yourself, and what's your least favorite?

How would an author describe you if they were introducing you as a character in a book?

_____

_____

_____

_____

_____

_____

_____

_____

_____

_____

_____

_____

_____

_____

_____

_____

_____

If you could be an amazing writer but it meant you couldn't do even simple maths, would you accept? What about the reverse?

Describe your typical day using bullet points.

Write a description of your bedroom as if it were for an alien - explain what everything is and what it's used for.

_____

_____

_____

_____

_____

_____

_____

_____

_____

_____

_____

_____

_____

_____

_____

Make a list of things you want to do before you turn 20.

Which celebrity would you have dinner with if you could? What would you say to them?

Would you rather be stuck in a lift with your best friend, or spend a day at the beach with your worst enemy?

Write about the last thing that made you smile.

What activity would you do if you were brave enough? Mountain climbing? Deep-sea diving?

Which bad habit would you most like to change? What would life be like without it?

Describe your ideal self at 25 years old. Where do you live? What do you spend your days doing?

If you could give $10k to any charity, which would you choose? Why?

What route would you take on your dream road trip? Write about where you'd go and what you'd do.

List the wonders of the world you'd love to visit one day.

Write about your current morning routine, and then your ideal morning routine.

_____

_____

_____

_____

_____

_____

_____

_____

_____

_____

_____

_____

_____

_____

_____

_____

_____

What would you do if you had ten 5-year-old kids to entertain on a rainy day? How would you keep them happy?

Which season is your favorite, and why?

If you could start a podcast on any topic, what would it be? Who would you interview?

What do you spend the most time worrying about? Will it matter in 5 years' time?

If you could only listen to one playlist for the rest of your life, which songs would you include?

_____

_____

_____

_____

_____

_____

_____

_____

_____

_____

_____

_____

_____

_____

_____

Which books do you think everyone should read at least once?

If you could bring back one cancelled TV show, what would it be? Why?

Would you like to live alone in a cabin in the forest? Why, or why not?

What's the biggest secret you're keeping right now?

_____

_____

_____

_____

_____

_____

_____

_____

_____

_____

_____

_____

_____

_____

_____

Which three things would you grab if you had to leave your home during a fire?

_____

_____

_____

_____

_____

_____

_____

_____

_____

_____

_____

_____

_____

What was your favorite thing to do when you were 6 years old? What's your favorite thing now? How are they different?

_____

_____

_____

_____

_____

_____

_____

_____

_____

_____

_____

_____

_____

_____

If you could live inside a video game, which game would you choose? Why?

What's your dream job? What's one small step you can take towards it today?

_____

_____

_____

_____

_____

_____

_____

_____

_____

_____

_____

_____

_____

_____

_____

_____

Think of an area in your town that needs improvement - what would you put there if you could?

Describe yourself from the point of view of someone you know.

_____

_____

_____

_____

_____

_____

_____

_____

_____

_____

_____

_____

_____

_____

If you could change, add, or remove one rule in your home, what would it be? Why?

You find an abandoned house in the woods. How do you turn it into a cool space to hang out in?

What if you could have 500k followers on social media, but none of your friends could follow you? Would you accept?

If you could be an expert on any topic, what would it be? How would you use your knowledge?

What's the weirdest dream you've ever had? What happened?

Do you believe in anything magical or supernatural? Why, or why not?

If you could create your own candle with any scent in the world, what would it be? Fresh grass? Old books? Baking bread?

Do you think books or movies are better? Why?

If you could go backstage at any concert, which would it be?

What's your favorite thing about modern technology? And your least favorite?

_____

_____

_____

_____

_____

_____

_____

_____

_____

_____

_____

_____

_____

_____

_____

_____

Which color do you think represents you best? Why?

Is there a strong opinion you used to hold, but don't any longer? What changed your mind?

Made in the USA
Monee, IL
02 November 2024

69200860R00056